Phrases, Poetry, and Prose

Anthony Eugene Hill

Phrases, Poetry, and Prose

ISBN 978-0-9853371-3-1
Copyright 2014 by
Anthony Eugene Hill
Montgomery, AL 36116

Contact Anthony Hill @
anthill31@hotmail.com

Printed in the United States of America.

All rights reserved under International Copyright Law. Contents and/or cover may not be reproduced in whole or in part in any form without the written consent of the Publisher.

Acknowledgements

Thank you God for giving me this gift and many others. I promise to use them for Your glory.

Thank you Lessie Garcia for guiding me through the publishing process and giving me sound advice.

Thank you Karen Frazier for your encouragement and editing.

Thank you Claude J. Collins, Jr. (CJ) for the cover design. It really represents the message I want to convey to my readers.

Thank you Bishop Kyle Searcy for always exhorting your

congregation to move forward, pursue, and walk through the open door.

Introduction

Over the years, I have developed some sayings that I have used daily during my tenure as a school teacher and/or in conversation. I want to share these words with you. I believe you will enjoy these fresh, coined phrases. In addition, I have included my poems and prose for your delightment.

THE PHRASES

The Bus
School Supplies
D.R.G.G. (DRAG)
Looking Good
No Burger King
You Can't Fool Me
Hallway Procedure
The Three B's
Classroom Video Games
The "Well" Clause
My Price
My Payment Methods
My Tests
One Line
Social Networks
Authority
Hanging Around the Restroom
Family
Your Seat
Best

G.O.
Get Along Gang
Don't Test Me
Don't Be Fashionably Late
Polo
N.O.N.E.
WWW
KB/KB

The Bus
Don't make a fuss
Get your behind on a bus
That's a must!

When dismissing students to get on the bus, they seem to want to meet briefly with their peers. This act makes it difficult for us teachers because we are trying our best to get them away from the school campus to their homes. It is time for them to leave us alone, so we may have some peace and quiet.

School Supplies
Get your need
Not your greed

In my classroom, I had a designated space called the student center for pupils to partake of anything they needed for class while they were with me. Sometimes, a few of the students would get more than what their eyes could behold.

D.R.G.G.
Drop it
Release it
Get up and Get out!

I had always ensured that my "babies" went to the restroom to do just that and nothing else. Time is of the essence, and I did not want them to spend wasted time talking in the lavatory.

Looking Good
If you don't look good now,
You will never look good

Students have a habit of grooming themselves too much throughout the day. They have a self-centered complex about their appearance. So, I would kindly remind them that the makeup kits, combs and brushes, et cetera should be done elsewhere, not here at school.

No Burger King
This is not Burger King,
You can't have it your way

Not to be slighted as a dictator, I wanted my students to know that I am in charge. What I say goes and that's final! When my students have earned the right to run their own classroom, that's when I will submit to their authority.

You Can't Fool Me
You can't fool the fool
You can't out slick the slickster
Or trick the trickster
In other words, there is nothing new under the sun. I have been there and done that. I am sure I have the t-shirt, pocket watch, wristband, and underwear for whatever stunt a student may try to pull on me.

Hallway Procedure
Quiet!
Teachers are teaching
Students are learning
Somewhere in the world
A child's pants is burning

    I am absolutely positive many of you would agree with me that silence is much needed in our classrooms unless some type of interactive activity demands noise. However, noise does not have a place in the hallway. Hallways are meant for passing, not conversing. When a class is loud and obnoxious, no one should know that it is yours being unruly throughout the corridors. Teach your children respect when they are within buildings of any kind.

The Three B's
Be quiet
Be seated
Begin bellwork

Upon entering a classroom, students should always have a lesson waiting for them to complete as they are taking their seats. Leaving a child with nothing to do is basically handing them over to Satan. An idle mind is the Devil's workshop. Structure the environment and there will not be any room for the occurrence of unnecessary circumstances.

Classroom Video Games
PSP – participate, study, and pay attention
Wii – we are intelligent individuals

Motivate your students! Be creative in how you want to achieve good results in your classroom. Familiarize yourself with things your students enjoy and use every tool to your advantage.

The "Well" Clause
Read well,
Write well,
Speak well,
And you will get a job
That pays well!

We want our students to become employers as well as employees. This message can only be achieved by giving our pupils the essentials that our society demands.

My Price
I do not pay their price
I pay my price

Be a good steward over everything in life. You should not pay what other people pay. Use coupons, look for discounts, bargain, negotiate, and wait for future deals. Do not spend your money haphazardly.

My Payment Methods
CDC: Cash-Debit-Check

Watch your pocketbook and purse. You should not be crediting your life away. Like the Bible tells us, "Owe a man nothing except love." You were made to prosper and to teach others this way of staying out of debt. Your wallet is a reflection of you!

My Tests
If you don't pass my test,
You are a hot mess!

I do not consider my exams to be difficult. Taking notes, paying attention, and studying will always eliminate the problem of failing one of my tests.

One Line
One line - You are not a two-headed monster

Passing through a narrow hallway can be tedious if one is taking up all the space. Keeping to one side allows someone else to pass on the other side. This world is big enough for all of us to move around in it. It wasn't designed for one person.

Social Networks
I don't put my face in anyone's book
I have my own space
And I don't tweet

Though I have a Facebook account, I truly have never been a fan of social networking sites. The phone and person-to-person contact methods are more fulfilling to me. Hiding behind technology avoids people ever seeing and knowing the real "you."

Authority
This is a dictatorship
Not a democracy
And I am the dictator

Teachers, your school system has given you a classroom with your name on it. It is yours to manage. No student should ever wear the hat in your learning environment. He or she should find it a pleasure and an honor just to be in your presence. Remember, students are the guests in your room.

Hanging Around the Restroom
No prostitution – this is an educational institution

At school, there are no "red light districts." The restroom is not a rest stop for chatting. Students are to allow nature to take its course and keep moving back to the classroom for the pertinent conversations.

Family
Don't talk to my students at this table
We are family–everyone else is a stranger

Some problems are preventable if there are rules. Certain things in the cafeteria such as a food fight or a brawl do not have to happen if teachers would monitor their students and set guidelines.

Your Seat
Face the correct way in your seat
You are either studious or stupid
Which one are you?

Some manners are evident. Sitting appropriately in a desk is one of them. The desk is only turned one way for a reason - for you to remain that way while you are in it.

Best
Best doesn't mean perfect

Perfection is never achieved, but you can do your best or be the best that you can be at something.

G.O.
G.O. not only means go, but "get out"

Many times we need to go to places; however, other times, we need to get out of them.

Get Along Gang (G.A.G.)
Okay, get along gang
Let's get along

Your classroom may contain

various personalities, but everyone in that room can get along.

Don't Test Me
Don't test me for you will be graded

All teachers have had students to try them. Many students have failed in this attempt because they had forgotten who they were talking to.

Don't Be Fashionably Late
Be fashionable, but not late

Like your wallet, your wardrobe speaks volumes about

you, too. People tend to forget that you are late, but they do recall your outfit.

Polo
I wear Polo, not "Oh, no!"

Out of all the clothes that I enjoy wearing, I find Polo to be the best. It is classic, comfortable, chic, and cool. Other brands try to copy the style of Polo, but they fail to replicate. This brand is iconic!

N.O.N.E.
Never Over Nine Eat

Many Americans try to stick to this habit; sometimes they break it like I do. Overall, it is a good one to follow. It helps in maintaining weight. Furthermore, by the dawning of the next day, one's stomach is ready to devour food again.

WWW
Watch What You Wear

It is a misdemeanor to not style your clothes or to at least ensure they match. You are always in the public's view, so do not let them view anything less than adequate in your dress.

KB/KB
Kick butt, don't kiss butt

In this world, many people in high places/positions would love for you to submit to their every wish. However, think about your integrity as a person. You do not have to compromise your beliefs to achieve your goals and aspirations in life. If I were you, I would kick their butt before I would even attempt to kiss their butt!

THE POEMS

Idol Identity
If I Could Change the World
I Am a Black Man
How Could I Not Love the Lord?
I Remember Him
Here I Am Dear Lord
Innocent
No More
We Are Here Dear World
Woman of Woes
Rough Hands
Is This My America
I Am Ready to Be Loved
Mirror, Mirror
A Black Man's Dialogue to America
Brother, We Are One
Basketball
Someone Cares about You
Ode to a Healthy Heart

My Colorful Poem – Red
The Songs of the Lord
In the Deep Woods
I Am Ready to Be Loved

Idol Identity

I'm in love with you, just you
There is an aura about you that I
can't explain
I'm giddy because you chose to
encase me with your beauty
I consider it a blessing just to have
you all over me
This fine and rich African origin of
color is so savor
If I had the opportunity to change
anything, I wouldn't
A stain like mine is worth the
absorption
It doesn't matter how light or dark
the skin, it's all good
Every morning when I awake,
I thank God for this outer shell
Yes, I know I may sound a bit
arrogant, but I can't help it
It's a realization that I've come to

marvel and revere
I am just so overwhelmed to
know...
That I've been blessed to be black

If I Could Change the World

If I could change the world
where would I start and where
would I end
surveying this same question
in which man has discussed over
and over again
If I could change the world
first, I'll let it begin with me
and then convert it into what I want
it to be

If I could change the world
nations would never go unfed,

unclothed and unsheltered
Everything in my world would be
equal
not singling out the best over the
better

If I could change the world
crime would be unheard of
because every day people would
undress more ways of spreading
love

If I could change the world
I would want more races of color
to add to the rainbow of humans
here
who are getting along quite well
with one another

If I could change the world
no one would have to succumb to
bitter formalities

for the laws of God would rule
humanity
and not governments or any other
principalities

If I could change the world
I would refurbish a perfect society
where all would be like me
Young, happy and free

I Am a Black Man

I am a black man
I am aware of my heritage, my
culture and my history
I dwell in the deepest parts of
Egypt
where the heated sun shines upon
my skin which absorbs the rays
And across the heated desert, I can
see my carved image
on the pyramids built by my
ancient brothers
who lifted stone by stone and
smoothed cement upon cement
until my figure was completed

I am a black man
I am aware of my heritage, my
culture and my history
I dwell in Africa, O' my begotten
home

where my feet stepped upon dry,
soiled ground
good enough for my brothers to
plant
and in due season, enjoy a ripe
harvest
I was the hunter and not the hunted
but oh how I was taken away to
America
where I endured much suffering
and shame
being called trifling names in an
uncaring land

I am a black man
I am aware of my heritage, my
culture and my history
I knew the things of the white man
I did as the white man did
and I desired his white woman
but I loved my African queen

And when freedom's cry watered
me away from my taskmaster
I no longer had to hide my face and
hold my head down
but I looked up and became
receptive
to the arms of equality and justice

I am a black man
I am aware of my heritage, my
culture and my history

How Could I Not Love the Lord?

Jesus came to the earth
He gathered twelve men together
Each of them had the same mission
to go out and spread His word and
to tell the weary and the lost
bringing all into His fold
to a place where they'll rejoice
forever

I would fix my bed in Hell
if His story, His story, I couldn't tell
because of love so pure
and all my sins He endured
When I was sick, He healed me
and made me glad when I was
down
Oh, what a love I know I have
found

One day I will take my rest

as I sleep and wait for my Master to
wake me up
from a life of sin and pain
to delight in the joys of His world
Forever, there, I will sing of His
goodness
and forever praise His holy name

Now tell me, how could I not love
the Lord
How could I not love the Lord
He surrendered His very life
on that old rugged cross for you
and me

I Remember Him

A traveler from a distant world
surveyed the people that were
around Him
Some, more than others, needed
His special attention
Inevitably, it was His chief concern
to bring peace into their hearts
While dispersing wisdom, healing
the lepers, and raising the dead,
many criticized Him for His works
of devotion
Out of anger and misunderstanding,
religious extremists resented Him
and excommunicated Him from
their synagogues
The words He shared were so
gentle and authentic
No wonder news of His fame
spread abroad
Embraced by many and alluded by

others to their own skepticism
Abruptly, a mob of Centurions took
Him captive for no apparent reason
It is written that a cowardly king,
Pontius Pilate,
could not merit justice himself, so
the people became the judge of this
innocent man
"Free Barabbas! Crucify that
man!"
They hissed and shouted
Did they forget about the shameful
throwing of stones
and judging someone before
judging self?
The Stranger treaded through the
streets of Golgotha to Calvary with
a heavy cross weighing down His
now fragile body
Consequently, the burdensome
cross He upheld moved not one to
help Him except one kind soul

That day, three men were hung, but only one of them for the crime of love

Despite the pain and agony He was enduring on the cross,
the Man said, "Father, Father, forgive for they know not what they are doing"
Alas, His head bowed with the crown of thorns upon it

"Weeping may endure for a night, but joy cometh in the morning"

Mary and others came to anoint Him with oil and spices
They were amazed by the rolled stone at His tomb
"Where is He?" they cried out
An angel of the Lord said, "You will not find Him here.

He is with His Father in Heaven."

Yes, I remember Him
Not only do I remember Him, but I
know Him
His name is Jesus Christ

Here Am I Dear Lord

Here am I dear Lord
I give myself to Thee
No more shackles holding me
I'm Yours for all eternity

Take my sins away
For I commit to Thee today
I won't falter nor stray
Because the answer you gave was to pray

My spirit broke its silence to say
Thank You, Lord, thank You, Lord
For coming my way

Man, I no longer amuse
Once made me perplexed and left me confused
I was living a defeated life with everything to lose

Until You arrested my soul for You
to use
Praising You with my talents many
would abuse

You whispered to me in one ear
Words so true and honestly sincere
Holy is the key to get to God, the
Almighty

Innocent

He was born in a family where
religion mattered
He left home beginning to
experience life on his own
From what he had seen his feelings
where shattered

He was exposed to the ills of
society: drunks, punks,

queers, steers, hookers, onlookers,
et cetera
There was nothing left for him to
see, nothing extra

He was at a point in his life where
he wanted to give up
Feeling so empty like water that
had been spilled from a cup
Hurt, torn, abused and misled was
he
Things of this nature he could not
handle
whatever the cases seemed to be

But this is what he acquired from
being in different places
as he interpreted the expressions on
people's faces

Soon he departed from this world
as it is meant

But one thing you could remember
about him
from the cradle to the grave, he was
always considered innocent

No More

No more
No more restraints
No more limitations
No more restrictions
Who's to say
What's this and what's that
Gosh
You get tired of the mess, things
and a whole lot more – people
Ugh!
Thank You, Lord for rest
for Your comfort
and in knowing who You are

Whew! Lord, where would I be
Stand in silence on some things
And will continue to stand in silence
It's a phase, and then it's not
Sometimes silence is a good thing
Yeah, it's a good thing
You don't have to give an answer
No questions to respond to
Thank You, Lord
Whew!

We Are Here Dear World

We are here dear world
Take us into your fold
For our minds are rich and new
Ready to vanquish the old

For we have studied hard
And crammed for many tests

Employ us dear world
And we promise to give you our
very best

We are here dear world
Awaiting and anticipating your call
To be committed to the challenges
Of the community, the
environment, and to be servants to
all

Lean on us with your problems
We have the answers, yes we do
If you can believe in Clinton's
cabinet
Then you can believe in us, too

We are here dear world
With no seniority and prestige upon
our shoulders
But it will come in due time
As we become much wiser and

much older

We are no longer college bound
But we are bestowed with a degree
That is solid and sound

We know of your roller coaster rides
Its many thrills and its many furls
But again I say to you, we're ready
We are here dear world

Woman of Woes

Her appearance did not match that
of a sweet mother
It had shown years and years of
scarred beauty
Driven away by inner grief
No words did she speak nor did a
whisper seep from her broken lips
Drabbed and detached from the
essence of life was she
Yet the calmness in her strides were
pleasant and peaceful
Giving an account of her many
struggles
I understood her tranquil ways
For her past had been slammed
with hate girded up from deep
oppression which left her barren
only to enjoy life alone
Woman of woes never breathed
hope

And it was well-written in her
expressions
Work was burying her body which
explained why the wrinkles on her
face were so explicit
No one revered the woman of woes
for she was too withdrawn
As she remained a hostage behind
doors of shame letting no one help
her escape the ton of misery that
held her down

Rough Hands

Rough hands, tiring hands, O' those
labouring hands of his
Hammering down hot, wrought
iron
Building buildings with bricks
plastering them with cement
While he lived in houses made out
of churned plywood
Picking cotton from the vast field
of his taskmaster's plantation
Fighting for freedom for slavery
was inhumane and too intolerable
Dying with dignity for his pride
surpassed white prostration
That's why I loved daddy's rough
hands, tiring hands, labouring
hands

But still, there were those rough
hands, tiring hands, and labouring

hands of hers
Scuffling to pay bills with nothing
but pennies to spare
Turning fatty chunks of leftover
pork into a variety of specialties
Cleaning the homes of others for
she was too jaded to clean her own
Praying on bending knees for the
betterment of her race
Nurturing valuable traditions and
ethics into her children
Who perpetuated her legacy as she
watched from above
That's why I loved momma's rough
hands, tiring hands, labouring
hands

But still, there is a need for more
rough hands, tiring hands,
labouring hands, what about your
hands?

Is This My America

Born to lead
Born to bear another seed
To perish in the U.S. Army
Not as a captain, but as a doggone
PFC

By some form of proclamation or
decree
Why want policymakers let things
be
It was not the Framers' U.S.
Constitution that made us free
It was God's grace and mercy, don't
you see

Moses and Martin were forerunners
of yesterday
Who minimized the number of
stumbling blocks put in our way
Yet, there are others many can't

recall today
Because false teachers have led
them astray

You may say this is not my battle
nor my fight
But I haven't heard one activist
complain of losing his or her life
It is true Congress doesn't seem to
hear the voices of certain races
Even though the Senate and the
House represent all these familiar
faces

As the increased understanding of
human needs and wants become
more visible
The respect we have for each other
is less congenial
This could explain why the Jews
and the Muslims are
"separate entities"

All to themselves, united as friends
and not divided as enemies

Is this my America
I undoubtedly have to ask
Is this my America
Yes, the place where I wear the
mask

I Am Ready to be Loved
(an "I" poem)

I am ready to be loved

I am ready for a relationship
I understand it really does take two
to tangle
I enjoyed solitude for a while
I now want the companionship of
another

I am ready to be loved

I do not want to live my life alone
I desire someone else to share me
I want to be happier than I am
I need you, whoever you are
I know life is sweeter when it is
complemented with someone else

I am ready to be loved

Mirror, Mirror

Mirror, mirror on the wall
Who is the vainest of them all
I know it has to be me
Because I am so fine and so sexy

Mirror, mirror I love your view
You make me look good and all brand new
Is this really me?
Tell me, please do

Mirror, mirror how is my face
Is it pale and wrinkle or is it still in place?
Mirror, mirror, a gift of mine
Remember, I am the one you should speak of all the time

Mirror, mirror how can I thank you
As I go on my way, farewell and

adieu
Mirror, mirror if you should ever crack
Your pieces I can't put back
But I will replace you just like that

A Black Man's Dialogue to America

I hear what America is saying about me
I'm nothing; I'm worthless
An epidemic of a terrible disease
Unpopular in society don't you see

I hear what America is saying about me
But I can turn things around
Putting me back on the map
Standing on a firm and unshakable

ground

I know America, you are outraged
But I'm neither afraid nor upset
For God, He isn't through with me
yet

America, when will you learn that
enough is enough
It was you who said that I'm mean,
lowdown and tough

America, you have accused me of
your most heinous crimes
But the tables are turning and now
it is my time
My time to do away with myths
and genocide
And regenerate a new America
where all can peacefully abide

Brother, We Are One

Why do you laugh at me?
What's wrong with me?
Am I not your brother?
I'm black just like you - I fear what
you fear
Tell me, why am I so different?
I am not any better than you or any
wiser

When you hurt, I'm hurting
When you cry, I'm also crying
I don't understand...
Why do you perceive me as your
enemy and not your friend?
Do you not know "together we
stand, divided we fall"?
Whether you know it or not
I'm oppressed by the same
ignorance that segregates all black
males of society:

rejection, humiliation, racism, and bigotry

Brother, we agree these are only mere forms of hatred that affects us both
Understand me when I say, "I need you"
I need you to stand with me and not against me because...
I can't say no to drugs if you're giving them to me
I can't become successful if you're hindering my progress
I can't be your ally as long as you consider me the adversary
I can't move if you're standing still
Brother, I can't rest until we are one

Basketball

Swish! Swish!
Goes the nets
Yeah, those are the boys
Who play on the NBA's basketball
teams
Watch them dribble
Up and down the court
Every turn and twist they make
Is a determinant to win the game

Up he goes into the air
For another shot
Slam dunk is what he did
All of the running, gliding
And striding motions are tiring
For the players on the court who
are all perspiring

Hey, the game has ended
With a winner and of course a loser

One taking home the trophy
And the other criticisms from the coach

Someone Cares about You

Avoid **carelessness**
But be **careful**
A lot of **careless** students
Did not make it back
But the ones who **cared** did

However, take **care** of yourself this spring break
Because someone **cares** about you
That is...I **care**

Ode to a Healthy Heart

Pump, pump your red blood
Let it flow through my veins
I am energized by you
My friends and families just the same

No cells, no ventricles
How would I survive?
O' healthy heart of mine
It's you who keeps me alive

My Colorful Poem – Red

Red is everywhere
It is on an apple, in my blood, and in that girl's hair!
Yeah, I often feel "red" when I'm angry
Just like the peak of a thermostat, wouldn't you agree?

Christmas is red – Santa Claus, mistletoes
And a combination of ribbons and bows
Even a hospital's symbol is red – the cross
For this color is so strong
It represents one in charge – the boss

The Songs of the Lord

The songs of the Lord
They are in the air
The songs of the Lord
They are everywhere

The songs of the Lord
These ballads I want to sing
The songs of the Lord
Personally, they mean everything

The songs of the Lord
I want to grasp
The songs of the Lord
To have one, all I have to do is ask

The songs of the Lord
I will write them
The songs of the Lord
Aren't they to Him, for Him, and about Him?

The songs of the Lord

In the Deep Woods

Night fright
Brings about a tasty delight
For hungry carnivores not in sight
Whose chore is to kill before
daylight

Pray you may
Live to see today
As human flesh okay
And not as cowardly dead prey

An owl's hoot
Signals the moment to panic or to
shoot
As you cringe to sounds all around
Allowing yourself to be idled with
the ground

Crickets in the thickets
Tuning against fence pickets

Making noise
Promising relief and a sigh for joy

Away from midnight's wrath
You stumble upon a path
Escaping the lure
Of what could have been an
unpleasant aftermath

The Prose

How We See Our Lives
It Was All in Their Music

How We See Our Lives

From the beginning, we open our eyes into a world from which we cannot turn back.
Moving forward and forward into life, images and people enlighten our minds as the hypothalamus records this information into our brain.
Colors beautiful...Weather changing...Human and animal transformations...
Even though these things are perpetual, the zest for life is timely.
As we race with time, the two-mile run doesn't seem as long as it used to be.
Yet, a few of us are still pacing in circular motions around life's track, not ever wanting to leave that which is now behind us.

Youthfulness gone...The sixteen candles blown...Marriage still holding strong...The children out on their own... -
a pattern throughout time man has been accustomed to.
Now, old age takes center stage as the years of adolescence fades behind the curtains of maturity.
Meanwhile, we patiently wait for that old ship of Zion to take us home.
And this my friends is how we see our lives.

It Was All in Their Music

It was all in their music: the rhythm, the beat, the harmony, and the voices. This special mixture coupled together forming the sounds of slavery. As hundreds of African slaves came to America, their music began to take on new forms, growing and expanding into the various kinds of music we hear today.

We hear spirituals. This type of music is sung mostly a cappella. They tell us stories about our history, from where we once were and up to where we are now.

We gave thanks to our Lord through gospel. Gospel means "good news." Its purpose is to inspire one to rejoice, praising God. It is accompanied by the additional movements of hand-clapping, foot-stomping, and spirit-filled holy dancing.

When we were down, the blues with its soothing and mellowing beats, reminded us of how depressed and miserable we were after having a discouraging fight with our mate. Its usual listeners are a crowd of lonely and brokenhearted lovebirds.

However, we were exhilarated by the jingling jamboree of jazz. It is a selective collection of orchestrated instruments. Sometimes, a few of the instruments would make their own personal debut like the trumpet, the bass violin, the drum, and the stringed guitar.

Because of the versatility of the young, they incorporated all the other mentionable music styles into rap, a wave of funky, hip-hop music. It is aided by the MC or microphone controller who does all the talking and on some occasions, beat boxing. His alias companion, the DJ, scratches and mixes records on the turntables.

Our forefathers brought within them a unique gift for all African Americans to share and to perfect. This is how they abstractly had fun in an unfriendly environment that cared little about their prosperity. Though they were slaves and enslaved by society, they were free through their music.

www.ingramcontent.com/pod-product-compliance
Lightning Source LLC
Chambersburg PA
CBHW071413040426
42444CB00009B/2226